Pain Is The Ink

Diane Wright

WestBow Press books may be ordered through booksellers or by contacting:

WestBow Press
A Division of Thomas Nelson & Zondervan
1663 Liberty Drive
Bloomington, IN 47403
www.westbowpress.com
1 (866) 928-1240

ISBN: 978-1-9736-6334-8 (sc)
ISBN: 978-1-9736-6333-1 (e)

Print information available on the last page.

WestBow Press rev. date: 07/11/2019

In this world you will have tribulation,
but be of good cheer. I have overcome
the world. John 16:33 (NKJV)
"I am the Way the Truth and the Life."
John 14:6 (NKJV)

Dedication

This book is dedicated to the One who I have come to trust more and more. More than anyone else. I know He loves me unconditionally and He wants me to be happy. He wants the best life for me. He wants that for everyone. I am so grateful to Him and I am grateful that we have His Word to guide us through this life. I hate to think of where I would be without Him. He is my Savior and sweet Heavenly Father... our sweet Heavenly Father.

Most importantly....

He said He would never leave me....

....nor forsake me.

Hebrew 13:5 (KJV)

Contents

My husband abandoned our family on July 9, 2016 (two days after our 25th anniversary), life become so very heavy....almost too heavy to bear. After he left, my sweet family and friends came to the rescue with their hard-earned money, support, food, gas cards, lawn mowers, new tires, coffee/grocery care packages, cards full of encouragement, beauty items (a definite luxury, and so appreciated), and special times "out to eat." Someone kept the propane tank full. It stayed warm inside, when it was cold outside. Family and friends came and helped me with my yard. They helped me remove limbs, leaves and removed dead trees that were laying in my yard. A couple of friends paid to have my yard mowed for a while until I regained my strength and got my bearings. They also helped me find extra jobs or provided jobs. Now, someone mows my yard for me, at no charge. They are saving me money and hours of my time. I'm overwhelmed at people's kindness and their love. I'm truly grateful to each of them. These wonderful people in my life can never truly know what they mean to me.

I don't know what I would have done without each of them.

They kept me from drowning.

~~ ~~ ~~

TO ALL OF YOU.

Thank you with all of my heart.

Introduction

The fact that you're reading this book is evidence that ANY situation that you are facing can change, if you put your HOPE in GOD and DON'T QUIT.

This is my story of a very difficult time in my life. A time when everything seemed to be going wrong and I was facing impossible situations. Feeling afraid and hopeless and sometimes worthless, I found myself just wanting to give up. Then, I thought to myself, "Where will that get me, but NOWHERE!" At least, if I don't quit, there is a chance I will make it! Doing what I knew to do and drawing my strength and hope from the WORD of GOD, I found hope and strength that, not only got me through this hard time, but brought me to a place of things being BETTER than I ever thought they could be.

After reading "Pain Is the Ink," I hope it will encourage and strengthen you as you GO THROUGH and GET THROUGH your difficult time.

~ *Diane Wright*

The pages hear, the pages listen,
The pages speak.

As I write what my heart feels
The pages are quiet – They listen so well.

Until it's their turn to speak
Then the story they'll tell.

TRUST

***Trust** is the firm belief in the reliability, truth, ability, or strength of someone or something.* There are those people in life that you know you can truly trust. You know you could count on them for anything. *Time and experience reveal someone's trustworthiness.* **Trust is such a valuable thing.**

There are those times, though, that only trust in God will do. There are situations that no one can fix. There are no words that anyone can say that will make things better. *You just need a miracle!* That is where I found myself from mid 2013 thru 2014. This is the year that I will remember as the second worst year of my life. Things had been rough financially for a very long time and it was affecting every area of our lives. There was nothing that the people in my life could do, so I didn't want to share any of this with them. It would just cause them to worry. Also, I knew, at this point, I couldn't bear the thought of listening to my dire state as I told anyone about it. It made me physically sick. I always thought that I trusted God, but this would be the ultimate test. I prayed, "God help me with this impossible situation. You're my ONLY hope." After I prayed, the words of the poem, "Do You Trust Me" came to me. God comforted me with these words and, somehow, I knew everything would be ok.

Do You Trust Me?

Do you trust Me.....
  When I said I'll take care of you
  Each and every day.
  When I said, I will protect you
  When you walk along the way.

Do you trust Me.....
  When I said, I will provide for you
  And give you all you need.
  Do you trust Me with the pain you feel
  That only I can see.

Do you trust me.....
  With your family
  The one's you hold so dear.
  Do you trust Me with your future
From your view – it is unclear.

— *It's clouded with uncertainty* —
— ***But mostly, it is fear*** —

Do you trust Me.....
  When I say My plans for you are bright.
  And If you stay close to Me
  Everything will be alright.

Do you trust Me.....
  When I say I will deliver you
  And I won't leave you all alone.
  And if you wander off from Me
  I'll come get you and lead you home.

If you trust me, you'll let go
So, I can take control.
I can't work things out for you
Unless you let them go.

TRUST is a VALUABLE thing
It has to be tested, proven and tried.
Test Me, prove Me, try My word
I'll pass the test each time.

Do you trust Me.....
When I say I'm coming back real soon?
Remember, there's no one in the world
Who loves you like I do.

Do you trust Me?.......

Yes, I do.
......and thanks for
loving me.

PAIN/LOSS

January 14, 2015

It was one year ago today that my nephew passed away. He was 27 years old. My mother called me on January 7, 2014 and said he was on life support. I knew it was very serious, but I just really thought that he would pull through. He passed away January 14, 2014. There are those things that we don't understand, but one thing I **do know** is that right now he is in the best place he's ever been (Heaven), and I **know** he is happy. This is not a permanent separation. We will see him again!

Loss is so painful. If you have experienced loss, I am truly sorry.

My prayer for you is that, if you have lost someone, that you will draw comfort from the Lord. A kind of comfort you will only find in Him. Let Him be your strength.

Isaiah 12:2 (KJV) ...the Lord God is my strength and my song, and He has become my salvation

Our Pain – Their Gain

When we lose someone
That we love so very much
When we miss hearing their voice
Or miss feeling their special touch.

A pain comes that's indescribable
Then the tears flow down our face
If we could just see them one more time
If we could feel their warm embrace.

But then....

We must remember!
If they're with our precious Lord.
They're not hurting – there's no sorrow!
They'll be happy forevermore!

They're in a place that's so beautiful!
Our minds can't comprehend
The light and love that surrounds them.
Will never, never end.

He is actually home
And will be waiting there for us.
For the time that we will come
He just got there first

It seems as though he left too soon
But now it is his gain
We're glad for him – but sad for us
God will help us with our pain.

So just like him
You must make sure
To "say it" and "believe"
In Romans 10:9 &10 – that is how it reads.

So, make sure that you confess
That Jesus Christ is Lord
Believe it – and be saved!
That's what opens Heaven's door.

If we ensure our place in Heaven
By coming the way God says
Then when we're in Heaven, together with each other.
We will never be separated again.

Romans 10:9-10 (KJV)

In memory of my nephew

August 30, 1986 – January 14, 2014

WORRY

I found myself worrying more than I ever had at any other time in my life. I knew better. I know worrying is not healthy and it never changed anything for the better. There were so many things during this season that went wrong, that worrying seemed to be the first place I would go. I was tired and became weary. I saw it physically take a toll on me. I was also being disobedient to the Word of God by worrying. One morning, I was already exhausted by worry and I thought, "I just can't do this anymore." Then words from scripture flooded my mind. "BE ANXIOUS FOR NOTHING. BELIEVE – DON'T WORRY." God said to be anxious for nothing! Believe. That seems to be a very tall order, but God's thoughts are higher than our thoughts. He knows best!

If you find yourself worrying, take your concerns to God, ask for HIS help and leave it with Him. If He tells you to do something, do it. He is capable of helping you. Worry is not! Take a chance and trust Him.

Philippians 4:6 (NLT) Don't worry about anything, instead, pray about everything. Tell God what you need, and thank Him for all He has done.

Believe – Don't Worry!

I can't worry anymore – I must believe!

If worry has become a way of life
For you most every day.
You have to realize right now
There is a better way.

For worrying gets you nowhere!
At least not where you want to go
Worrying usually makes you sick
And will send you down the wrong road.

If you're worrying – You're not believing!
God says you won't get anything that way
Be not afraid – ONLY BELIEVE1
God's perfectly capable to save.

He'll save you if you're lost
He'll save you if you're sick
He'll save you if you're broke
If your focus on Him stays fixed.

If you turn your focus to anything else
Your outcome has no guarantee,
But the focus on Jesus and all that He says
Every time brings VICTORY.

If you're tired from worrying
And you just want to be at peace
Make a decision.....stop worrying.
Make a decision.....just believe.

What are you worrying about?
Believe in God – Don't worry

OBEDIENCE

Lord, Will You Meet Me At The Edge?

Will you meet me at the edge
If I choose to go that far
A place where few will venture
For fear that they will fall.

By the edge is very scary
But can also hold a glimpse
A glimpse of that miracle
That most in life will miss

The "edge" is the "place of the impossible"
A place of no turning back
If you're brave enough to go there
There seems to be no lack.

One "place of the impossible" was with Moses
When he was at the "edge" of the Red Sea
There was no lack for what he needed
There was dry ground as far as he could see.

What about the woman who went for Elisha
When her son had already died
What she said, was "all is well"
Most would have said she'd lied.
Her son did die, but she chose to believe....

........then he was ALIVE!

There's Peter that walked on the water
And Daniel who prayed unashamed
When the pit was opened the next morning
Hungry lions looked nothing but tame.

The edge of the fire in a furnace
Is where you meet three Hebrew men
Their clothes didn't smell like smoke
Their hair not even singed.

Lord, it seems that you'll meet anyone
Willing to go to the "edge" for You
Thanks for answering my question with Your Word
I know now you'll meet me there too.

The edge is a different place
For each of us in life
Lord, give me the courage to go to the edge
With You for a better life.

So, no matter what the "edge"
In life will be for you
You can be sure, if you trust in God
God will meet you there too.

~ "The edge" – Total Obedience To God ~

~~~

Fight for what you know is right.

Never stop fighting.

Protect those you love.

Let the one's you love
know they're worth fighting for.

~~~

Fight

If it's worth it – fight for it!

When you go to bed
And don't hug me goodnight
When you leave in the morning
And don't say good bye.

When there's no closeness between us
For years at a time.
And a kiss on my lips
Is just a faint memory in time.
.........It makes me sad.

I long for a love
That doesn't change with a mood
To feel secure and protected
I want to feel this from you.

For me, you've never stepped up
To the plate
When one has attacked me
With words filled with hate.

I think there's a fine line
That we haven't found yet
Between "keeping the peace"
Or just being "a door mat."

Anything worth having
Is worth any fight
Or you'll lose it forever
And that wouldn't be right.

Whether it's your health or your home,
Your family or wife
Only you can answer
Is it worth the fight?

DESPERATION

I Was Desperate

You were there for me.
.....and I'll never doubt you again.

Lord, I'm desperate for Your mercy
I'm desperate for Your grace
These are the only things that will help
With this devastation that I face.

This is one true test
That will prove to me You care
Like a loving father
Who says he'll always be there.

Be there with arms wide open
Ready to wrap me in Your love
And tell me "It will be ok."
And, I can rest...because, YOU, I can trust.

Trust that what You tell me is true
And that all my needs You will supply
Trust You because you're the ONE
Who says, He cannot lie.

I want someone who is there for me
Father, will you help me work this out
(Heavenly) Dad, if you can get me through this
Never again, IN YOU, will I doubt.

PURPOSE/YOUR MISSION

-

Ecclesiastes 12:13 (KJV)

....Fear God,
and keep his commandments:
for this is the whole duty of man.

WORSHIP GOD.

Whatever He tells YOU to do,
DO IT.

John 2:5 (NASB) His mother said to the servants,
"Whatever He says to you,
do it."

Your Mission

I remember one day we were talking
And you said, "What is my mission in life?"
I've heard many ask the same question
It's also been a question of mine.

I pondered on that a while
And a few thoughts have come to mind.
Your mission is "being you"
Time to complete it is "your life time."

Everyone's mission is different
We must be careful not to compare.
Because each mission is important
The same mission we do not share.

Sometimes the mission is big
Sometimes it is very small.
For the "Main Mission" to be successful
It doesn't take a few of us – but it takes us all.

I look at your life
And you've had many missions
One is being a mom.

A mom
That would do ANYTHING for us
A mom that is very strong.

I've seen how you help others
In so many ways…
I know you think those things are small.

But you may never know
What it means to someone
To take them dinner or to the mall.

You've always been a hard worker
And have always made a good home.
Even when "you think" you're home, not doing much
That means someone's not alone.

Your mission in life is to do everyday
All that you know to do.
The best way to complete that mission
Is just by "being you."

A BROKEN HEART

Psalm 34:18 (NLT), The Lord is close to the brokenhearted;
he rescues those whose spirits are crushed.

God's

Forgiveness

God's

Love

Mended Hearts

A mended heart was once broken
But now "love" fills in the "breaks."
The "breaks" were caused by many things
Which left the heart hopeless and filled with aches.

Many experience a broken heart
As they travel through this life.
But there is a substance that will fill the "breaks"
That will seal them up real tight.

There is a process, though,
To make sure the cracks stay sealed.
The heart has to be cleaned out first
For it to properly heal.

No matter how the heart was broken
The goal is for it, again, to be whole.
No matter what someone has done to us
To be happy and healthy is the goal.

Forgiveness is the first step
It's a choice – and hardest to apply.
But if this step is not taken
The heart will eventually die.

We must think of everyone
Who has caused our heart to break.
And 'choose' to forgive them
As we call them out by name.

Forgiveness is not deserved
It's 'given' to those who offend.
It's also necessary for us
If our hearts will ever mend.

After forgiveness
It's love that we apply.
It's the strongest bond available
A substance few ever really try.

Love is also a choice
It's not our own that we will use.
It's the perfect love of God
That will mend and strongly fuse.

"Our" love is conditional
We definitely need His help.
Ask God to love through you
Because "His" love never fails.

A mended heart was once broken
The bond of "love" filled in the breaks.
Over time you couldn't even see the cracks
A whole heart was in its place.

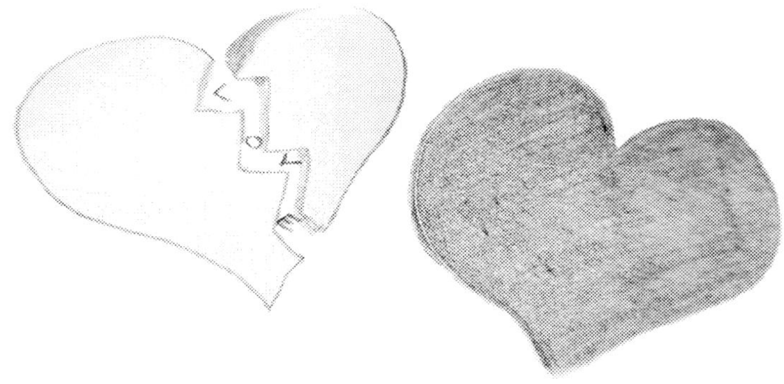

~ A mended heart was once broken ~

ENCOURAGEMENT

Psalm 89:9 (ESV) You rule the raging of the sea: when its waves rise, you still them.

Psalm 107:29 (KJV) He maketh the storm a calm, so that the waves thereof are still.

~ ~

If God can command the seas, I believe He can rule my life better than I.

~ D.W.

I turn the helm over to You, Lord.

Be the calm in me.

Sink or Sail?

"Sailing" through life is what people say
When things are going real smooth.
But they use the word "sink" when things get rough
And they don't know what to do.

I would say most of us have experienced both
I prefer "sailing" anytime.
But if you run through rough waters
Don't forget! There is a life line.

The life line is always available
So, when the winds begin to blow.
Make sure you're connected to the One
Who's called, "The Anchor of Our Soul"

The life line is Jesus
And He can always get you through.
Any storm that develops
He will be your refuge.

He will keep you steady
While the storm rages on.
When all around you is so boisterous
He can keep you calm.

When life seems to have taken
The wind out of your sail.
And every turn you take
Seems to be met by stormy gale.

Remember, Jesus is the One
Who can calm that raging sea.
Turn the helm over to Him
And SAFE, with HIM, you'll be.

Sometimes it's hard to know
How long each storm will last.
Stay connected to Him, so you won't "sink"!
And you will "sail" again at last!

You Make A Difference

You make a difference just by being here
You'll never know what your life means.
Your presence here on the earth
Is more important than you may think.

Sometimes the devil will tell us
That we don't matter much.
But he is such a liar!
To tell us things and such.

God made us all for a purpose
To carry out His plan.
To influence those around us
To extend His loving hand.

So, every day when you wake up
Remember this instead.
That you were formed by Almighty God
You are special. You're like a thread.

A thread sometimes is not noticed
But it holds together mighty things.
Like flags that fly majestically
Or garments of a King.

Each of us are important
We all have to be reminded sometimes.
Know that you are loved by so many
Life wouldn't be the same without your sweet smile.

You are making a difference in someone's life.
You matter.

READY TO GO HOME

She lived a good life
But it was coming to a close.
She must have known it was time
She's been saying "I'm ready to go home."

She's left her mark here
That's what we all do.
While we're here on earth
Just passing through.

The mark that we leave
Can be good or bad.
But the one that Gran left
Leaves us happy – not sad.

*   *   *   *   *

What a wonderful thing!
What a wonderful place!
The home that awaits us
To see Jesus sweet face!

To be reunited
With those who are there!
To experience God's presence
His glory's everywhere.

To see the brightness
That comes from His face.
To, again, see our loved ones!
To feel their embrace!

When she gave her life to Jesus
Her name was written down
In the "Lamb's Book of Life"
Where names of all "saved" can be found.

If your name is not there yet
Just simply say,
"Dear God, I give my life to you."
"In Jesus name I pray."

Then a place will be prepared for you.
Just like it was for Gran
We will all be together again.
Forever, safe in God's hands.

She will be missed
We loved her so
But we are happy for her
She was "ready to go home."

Written for my best friend's grandmother.

July 6, 2014 –

I've had this feeling for several days that I need to make sure my "slate" is clean with everyone - that everything is right with me and everyone that I know. I've thought about different things over the past several years. Things I've said to people. Not realizing then, but seeing how it could have been so hurtful. It makes me sad to think I would have hurt them. I've learned that when you are hurting you become so self-centered. I have been self-centered, so deep in my own hurt, that I didn't see some of those around me drowning in theirs. Lord, help those I was not there for. If you were one of those people, I'm so sorry. I do love you.

I've seen how years can pass and hearts stay broken. People don't talk. Time goes by. Time is wasted. Time is gone.

If someone has hurt you and it is something you just can't let go of, talk to them. Forgive them. Give them a chance to say they're sorry.

Life is too short.
.......let the healing begin.

Matthew 18:15 (NIV)

Have I Ever Hurt You?

Have I ever hurt you
With something that I said?
Have I ever hurt you
With something that I did?

If I have, I am sorry
From the bottom of my heart.
I know unhealed hurts
Are the reasons people part.

You are important to me
And I love you very much.
I think it's really important
For loved one's to stay in touch.

So, if I've hurt you
I'll take this time to say.
I am sorry – forgive me
For making you feel that way.

If someone's hurt you – talk to them
Give them a chance to say
"I'm sorry, please forgive me."
"I never meant to hurt you that way."

Let the healing begin……

RESTORATION

~ Love is stronger ~

~ Love is stronger than any mistake ~

~ Love is stronger than anything broken ~

"THIS PLACE"

How did we get to "this place"?
A place I never thought we would be.
You can't tell me what's bothering you
You used to share everything with me.

I feel like a part of me has been cut away
The place where you used to be.
But you are not there right now
I miss you and it crushes me.

I'm partly to blame
By things that I've said
And the way that I've said them to you.

But please always know
I never meant to be mean
I just want the best for you.

I wish I could erase all of our hurts
And things that were not so good.
But I can't – that is life, but one thing I do know
Is I'll never stop loving you.

I'm sorry for the part that I played
In taking us to "this place"
But I know the LOVE and BOND that we share
Is stronger than ALL the mistakes.

REASSURANCE

What God says is true. It is the only sure thing that will change a situation. A minister that I highly respect taught a message years ago entitled, "Speak the Word Only".

Every time I find myself in a difficult situation that definitely needs to change, those words ring in my ears.
"Speak the Word Only"
They are words that I need to be reminded of often.

Remember God changed everything with His words. He has instructed us to do the same. Stop believing the worst will happen and speaking only the negative. Speak the Word ONLY and watch your world change.

Genesis 1
(KJV)

What Happened when I said, "........"?

What happened when I said, "Let there be light."
There was light.....And it was good.
What happened when I said, "Waters gather together."
Yes, by the dry land the seas stood.

What happened when I said,
"Let the earth bring forth grass, herb and fruit tree."
What happened when I said to the waters,
"Bring forth abundantly!"

—You're right. What I said came to pass....and still is—

TODAY – There is still light.
There's still grass under your feet.
There's still cattle and fowl
Creatures still swim in the sea.

The same thing happens
Every time I speak.
Things are created
In Me, there is NO DEFEAT.

MY WORD is powerful!
It carries weight.
A weight that can crush
And a power that creates!

The fig tree could not live
When out of My mouth the words came.
When you speak MY WORD to your problem
It will do the same thing.

MY WORD creates LIFE
It can crush every disease.
Put it to work
And only believe.

Whatever the circumstance
The BEST is what I want for you.
Use only MY WORD
It will be your breakthrough!

Let My creation that surrounds you
Remind you of how.
Things change with MY WORD
Not just then – but right now.

SPEAK THE WORD ONLY1

Speak it! Change it!

Pain Is the Ink

Sometimes *Pain Is the Ink*
Used to write a song or a poem.
Sometimes no other ink can be used
To turn another's pain into joy.

For it's the experience of one
That can show another
A different way to go.

How can we help someone
If we've never been there?
How else would we know?

~~~

This ink is an expensive ink
It comes at a very high price.
Usually there is great loss
Perhaps possessions or someone's life.

It is very painful to be the holder of this ink
You don't want it at the time.
But, what if it could ease someone's else's pain
Maybe change someone's life.
~~~

There comes a time
When the ink is all gone
There's no writing left to do.

If you can help others
With the words you write
Then, the pain was worth going through.

Sometimes.....

Pain Is the Ink

COMFORT

Psalm 46:10 (KJV) says, "Be still and know that I am God."

Hebrews 13:5 (KJV) ...for He hath said, I will
never leave thee, nor forsake thee.

I KNOW YOU ARE THERE

(Sitting in my chair praying at home one evening)

I know You are there
Though I can't see Your face.
I know You are there
Even if I don't feel an embrace.

I know You are there
Listening to me.
I know You are there
Caring for me.

Someone may ask
How do you know He is there.
I feel His presence
Sitting here in my chair.

His presence is like a warm blanket
Or warm oil, or the sun on your face.
There is a peace that comes all around you
No other feeling can take its place.

Lord, You're always welcome
To stay here with me.
I know you'll never leave me.
It's you that I need.

GRANDMA ON LOAN AT THE CRACKER BARREL

January 5, 2014 –

Yesterday, my husband and I were planning on going to church, but I found myself taking care of a family matter instead. Since we would be late to church we decided not to go. They were having communion this Sunday morning and we did not want to walk in on the middle of it, so we decided to go to Cracker Barrel and eat breakfast. I was feeling pretty sad about having to deal with those issues that morning. I wished, at this point, these things wouldn't have to be dealt with anymore. I was wishing my children could have been there eating breakfast with us. I was really missing them. I was heartbroken. I so appreciated getting to be there with my husband, but I also found myself fighting back tears, thinking some of these things we were going through should not be this way. After we finished eating, we went to pay in the country store. My husband paid, then went to the car. I stayed to look around the store for a while. There is a lady that works as a greeter in the store. She is the sweetest lady. She has the most beautiful white hair and the kindest face and sweetest voice. I really enjoy visiting with her when we go to Cracker Barrel. As we were talking, she told me how her job was an answer to prayer. I felt a connection with her. When I told her she was a sweet lady, she said, "I'm really not – It's Jesus." What honesty! I knew why I was drawn to her. As we talked, I kept fighting back tears. Finally, I told her I had to stop talking to her or I was going to start crying. I didn't really want to cry in public. Then she said to me, "Whatever you are having problems with right now, in a year, it probably won't even be a problem anymore." I felt such comfort from her words. I asked her if she had children. She said she had three children and 12 grandchildren. She put it this way. "I have three children and their spouses are my children, too, and all their children are my grandchildren. What a loving and accepting comment. I want to have that attitude toward my children, their spouses and their children, whether they are biological or not. Her words eased my hurting soul that morning. Her kind words eased my pain. Even though I really don't know her, I felt as if we were very close for a few moments. I hugged her before I left and told her she had done me a lot of good. I felt like I was being hugged by a grandma and she was telling me everything was going to be all right. She says her job is a "God send." That day, for me, she was a "God send." This lady made a difference in my life!

January 18, 2015- 4:30 p.m.

I had to do something so hard today. I told my boss, my friend, I was not coming back to work in the spring. It made me SO sad. I have the perfect job, the perfect boss, doing what I love to do - being around flowers and being outside. They have been so good to me and I love spending time with them. I will miss not seeing them as much.

My head says, it makes no sense to leave, but my heart says this is right for this time.

I feel the need to write so many things down. There are so many other things that I'm doing and I have neglected to set aside the time needed for this project. I feel like at the end of my life, not writing would be a huge regret and an act of disobedience. I have put this on the back burner for some time and I think this has been the cause of some of the unrest and dissatisfaction I'm feeling. Today, I made a commitment to do my best to do what it takes to finish this assignment. In the middle of something like this, thoughts do come: "Does anyone really care what I have to say?"......Maybe, maybe not, but I know that I will do my best to finish what I feel has been given to me to do.

Follow Your Heart – Not Your Head

Following your heart doesn't always make sense to our head.

Acknowledge God in everything.

Be led by His Spirit.

Always follow the peace.

Be willing.

Be obedient.

Proverbs 3:6 (KJV) In all your ways acknowledge Him and He shall direct your paths.

Isaiah 1:19 (NIV) If you are willing and obedient, you will eat the good things of the land.

Romans 8:14 (NIV) For those who are led by the Spirit of God are the children of God.

Colossians 3:15 (AMPC) Let the peace of God rule your hearts, acting as an umpire;...

HEARTACHE

January 24, 2015

The phone rings early Saturday morning. My husband said the lady who bought our house said she was sorry for the short notice, but she would be there this morning with a contractor to make plans on building beside us. Sadness floods my heart. I was looking forward to a day I didn't have to rush to get around and now I have to get ready for company. I didn't have much to do, but still having to instantly worry about all of this was unnerving. It is a slap in the face and a painful whisper that at any moment someone can just show up at my home any time they wanted. It was just a grim reminder that, on paper, our home belongs to someone else. I prayed and tried to stay focused on what we are believing. (We are believing that we will own our home again soon and that it will be PAID IN FULL. I do want to be kind to people and I had wanted to have coffee with this lady on one of her trips to Denison, but it was just so hard under the circumstances. It didn't work out her last trip, so I thought we would try again this morning. After she finished with the contractors, she came up to the house. That was the first time I actually met her. I did enjoy the visit and for some moments I just got lost in the moment of meeting someone new and enjoyed hearing about her life. Then, reality would hit me in the next moment and I realized I'm sitting here with the owner of "my home," and she's talking about building on our property not knowing that where she is talking about building are the places that I've hiked and played through the woods with my children and built forts with my nephew. She doesn't know it, but as she sits here telling me of her plans to build here on our home property, and all of the rentals she owns, (mine is now one of them), MY HEART BREAKS. I have to trust the Lord, knowing that He has heard our cries and believe that though our situation looks impossible, He is going to work this out for our good.

A GRATEFUL HEART

Even though things can be really hard at times, there is so much to be grateful for. There will always be those who have more than you, but there are always those who have less. Thank you, God, that I have so much to be grateful for. I want to mention a few of them and just say "thanks."

I am so grateful that I am a mother and a mother in law and that my children are so loving and respectful. I'm grateful that we have a good relationship. I am grateful that I am a grandmother and a grandmother-to-be. I am grateful for so many things.

I'm so thankful for my family and my friends and the love we have for each other. I am thankful for my church and church family. I'm thankful that me and my family have a roof over our heads and food to eat. We have all been blessed with cars to drive. We are all in good health and able to work. Thank you for our jobs. We are also able to have animals. They pour their love out to us in their own special way.

I am most grateful for God, who is our good Heavenly Father, who makes life worth living. He cares for us.

I am grateful.

YOUR CHOICE

My mom rode with me to the dentist in Dallas today. I will have to make several trips. I have a lot of work that needs to be done. I am grateful that I am now able to get it done. I have enjoyed our time together in the car, in the cafeteria and taking mini tours through the hospital.

Thinking about the many conversations we've had today and things I read on the history of the hospital and some of the things the girl taking my X-Rays said, it's so evident that everything that we do in life – is a choice. I know there are those things in life that we do not have control over. I'm talking about those personal, everyday choices that are ours to make. We can decide what we will do for our careers, if we will act on that idea, in what condition will we get behind the wheel of a car, what kind of person we will bring home to meet mom. We can decide who we will marry. We decide what we will wear, where we will live…but even if you say you don't have a choice in these things I've listed, there are a few things that we ALL have a choice in, and these are really important. What attitude will you have? How will you treat those you run into today. (Especially those inside your four walls, those closest to you.) What words will you speak? Who will you not criticize or gossip about? Will you frown all day or try to smile? Even if you don't smile for yourself, smile for someone else. It will do them a lot of good. It will actually do you more good than you think.

The MOST IMPORTANT - who will you serve today? Joshua 24:15 (KJV) says, "Choose this day whom you will serve; …..but as for me and my house we will serve the Lord.'

I believe we can make our world a better place….one good choice at a time. Let's make some good choices today.

Choose

Choose this day who you will love
Choose this day not to hurt
Choose this day how you will live
Choose this day whom you will serve.

Choose what you hear
Choose what you say
These choices are OURS
To make EVERYDAY.

Will we choose to tell them the truth
When a lie would be easier instead
Will we choose to look up and hope
Or give up and hang our head?

It's not easy, I know
I have to make these choices, too.
But the choices are ours
We have the freedom to CHOOSE.

......choose well.

The worst year of my life.......

I have fought this moment many times. I did not want to relive any of what I'm about to write. I would have never written it down. I would have never shared this pain, if I could not have written an ENDING WITH HOPE. Even now, it's hard to write. Here it goes.

January 2014 will be ranked as the 2nd worst year of my life. The worst year in some ways. January started with the horrible news of my nephew. The call came January 9, informing me he was on life support. He passed away January 14. This didn't seem real. He was only 27. This shouldn't be happening.

Surrounding the time at the hospital, a time when we needed to all stay connected, my family's cell phones were cut off, due to nonpayment. Why now? The things that follow will never compare to the loss of my nephew, but were devastating, none the less.

On January 10 (right in the middle of my nephew's fight for life), there was a knock at my front door. I am met by a lady (a realtor) who informs me that my home has been put up "for sale," and they were starting eviction. I had no idea what was going on. We had a short time to move everything from a place that had been our home for 23 years. I was in shock. I just started shaking. She was very nice, but the news she delivered was paralyzing.

After she left, I went to my closet, closed the door and melted in the floor. All I could do was just groan as I sobbed and pleaded with God. I felt so alone. I was supposed to meet with my best friend that day. I text her and told her I couldn't make it. She asked me if I was ok. I remember just breaking into tears in the bathroom again as her words of concern came through text. She said she would pick me up and we would just drive around. She will NEVER know what that meant to me that day. She encouraged me, as she always does, but most importantly, she stood in FAITH with me. The only thing that would make a difference at this point. I NEEDED A MIRACLE. When she brought me back home, we got out of the car and she said, "We are going to walk over your property and pray," so she took my hand and she marched around the driveway and prayed and declared! I can't remember exactly what she said, but I felt peace, renewed strength and hope. What kind of friends you have makes a difference! What kind of friends do you have? What kind of friend are you?

Proverbs 18:24 (NIV) ....but there is a friend who sticks closer than a brother.

How it started.....

Income had not been steady for a long time. We had become behind on our house payments, but made arrangements with our mortgage company. I thought everything was fine. There were many times through the years that I thought everything was fine, but they weren't. I found fear and distrust trying to become my close companions. I didn't want to feel this way, but I was so afraid. I often had to fight the attitude. "What next?" On February 14, a few days after I received the news about our house being put up for sale, we were asked to come sign papers at the realtor's office. February 14th is also my mom's birthday. I remember meeting her at McDonalds that morning for coffee. That was the only thing I could afford to do for her that day. I had no money to get her a birthday present and I tried my best to hide what was going on and what I had to face that afternoon. That afternoon, on the way to the realtor's office, I was physically sick. When we got there, I told my husband I could not sign the papers. I would have to do it the next day. Later, we realized that God was protecting us. If we would have signed these papers, it would have been to our detriment. On February16, my dog (Roxy) got really sick. I thought she might die. She is very old and we have had her a very long time. I hated seeing her suffer. Under the circumstances, just another negative thing seemed like too much to bear. That day, I took "communion" alone. Over the next week, she improved. Then she was back to normal. I was so grateful. I thought, 'she just keeps going and going – like the energizer bunny.'

(I'm not sure why I put this in here. At this point, I guess I'm thinking I'm just sitting with someone, pouring out my heart to someone who cares to listen.)

On February 19, we filed for bankruptcy. We were told that was the only way to buy a little more time in our home. Not much time. Just a month or so. We felt that was our only option, at the time. I can't even put into words the hopelessness I felt. Years of our lives seemed like they were just going to vanish before our eyes. No home, no credit – nothing.

While we were at the attorney's office, getting the papers ready for the bankruptcy, they asked what our income was for the year. When we told him, "He said, is that for a month?" The thought of our income for a year being confused with a month's income was just another reminder of what poor shape we were really in.

I know people didn't understand why I never bought anything while shopping or bought grocery items when they were on sale in bulk or went to the doctor or dentist when it was needed. We had NO money. We would scrape up change to go to the grocery store sometimes. It was the kindness of family members and their sensitivity that kept our stomachs full at times. They wouldn't say anything about our situation – just, "I noticed I had extra of this" or "this was on sale, I had to get several." I appreciated them so much.

I wouldn't drive past Wal-Mart for days at a time, because we didn't have money for gas. Wal-Mart is only two minutes from our house. I felt trapped. I felt humiliated so many times. I have joked about it since, but it may have been good at the time that I didn't have gas – I may have left. There were times I wanted to.

During this time, people would say what are you doing? It looks like you're losing weight. I would be thinking in my mind. "It's the 'no food' diet." I guess I can look at that as a positive thing. That's one way to lose weight, and you don't even have to have will power. (That is one of those "laugh so you don't cry" statements.)

On February 28, we were served "eviction papers." To make things even worse, the constable went to our neighbor's house by mistake, so now they knew. My neighbor called me about it. I just said we were having an issue with the mortgage company, but hoping to get it worked out. Humiliation joined the devastation.

In March, I was getting gas by the mall. I had just pulled up and was about to pump my gas. My husband called and said, "our house was sold in auction." I could barely breathe. I didn't know if I could make it home.

I was devastated. I felt so alone. I was just numb. "Why, Lord?"

Days later…..

God's Mercy

We were informed that the first deal to buy our home, fell through. Then a lady from Nevada said she came across our home "by accident" and decided to buy it. This was NO ACCIDENT. She said that we could stay in our home for the rest of our lives. This could have already gone so differently. We should have been out of our home buy now. We are still here. This is our home. The house that my husband and his dad built. Every board was put in place by people I love. Birthday parties, proms, family gatherings. So many memories… I'm so grateful for my home.

The people that bought our home have been so kind, so gracious….I am so grateful for them. This is something that I can't deny that God had his hand in.

Because of this couple buying our home and saying we could stay as long as we wanted, we were able to cancel the bankruptcy. Thank God!
"God's blessings on this couple and their family."

Our home was actually paid off at one time, but we took a home improvement loan out on it to get water to our house from the highway and some other improvements. As we fell behind on the payments, we made arrangements with our mortgage company and they put us on a special program. I thought that we were in good standing with them. Then, all of a sudden, our house was sold. It seemed unreal.

Since then, my husband abandoned me, June 9, 2016, two days after our 25th anniversary. At this point, I really don't know the truth about my home and I'm not sure about many things. **I just know I need a miracle.**

I am asking God for wisdom and favor. I believe God is my vindicator and my defense. My desire is that I will own our home again soon. My earnest prayer is that I will have a good inheritance to leave to my children and grandchildren.

Psalm 4:2-4 (CJB) O God, my vindicator! Answer me when I call! When I was distressed, you set me free; now have mercy on me, and hear my prayer.

Psalm 94:22 (KJV) But the Lord is my defense; and my God is the rock of my refuge.

Proverbs 13:22 (NIV) A good person leaves an inheritance for their children's children.

GOOD ENDING PENDING…

MISTAKES

My husband left for Inverness, Scotland, May 11, 2015. Two months and 3 days had gone by and I had not been able to write one thing. I knew my heart wasn't right. There were times I felt so alone. I know wives of service men have been alone much longer, but their husbands don't have the option of taking them with them. I felt I was, again, just left behind, by choice, having to live life by myself. I was mad and sad. My kids and my family were great! They were there for me, I just felt me and my husband should have been together.

As the days went by, I tried to keep a good attitude, but I was really struggling this time with him being gone. If he is doing what God wants him to do, I really don't want him doing anything else. I wanted to be supportive, but for the first month I was just mad! Mad for being alone AGAIN, mad for doing things that I wouldn't be doing if my husband were home. Shoveling rock after the rains washed out some of our driveway. Having to kill scorpions while loading the trash to take to the road. Killing copperheads and tarantulas. Being home alone at night when I felt my husband should be with me. I know things could be so much worse, but, nevertheless, I was feeling somewhat abandoned. I accused God that it seemed He didn't care. I felt my only option was to just deal with it.

Don't ever do this! God is not our enemy. I knew better! One day I was outside watering and God kindly reminded me He was taking care of me in a lot of ways and we were in better shape than we were the previous times my husband went to Scotland. I truly want my heart to be right no matter what's going on in life. I went to God and repented – and said, "If you can still use me to write, I would be honored."

That night, even though I had messed up, I sat down
in my rocking chair and the words to the poem
"My Mistakes, God's Grace" came to me.
This is only one of MANY mistakes I've made, but God is so
loving, so forgiving and is just waiting on us to come to Him.
He will still use us, He will forgive us, He always loves us.
No matter what mistakes we've made, if we
are truly sorry, God will forgive us.

My mistakes, God's Grace

God, thank you for Your mercy
Thank You for Your grace
Thanks for still loving me
Even though I make mistakes.

Thank You for Your forgiveness
That covers all the "wrongs" I've done
You knew that the Only Way
Was the precious Blood of Your Son.

You knew it had to be precious blood
To pay the price for all
It had to come from the Spotless Lamb
It had to cover the cost.

His blood - It covers everything
That anyone's ever done
Just go to God and repent
He's just waiting for you to come.

God…He loves us more
Than we will ever know
Though our sins are like scarlet
He'll make them white as snow.

Isaiah 1:18 (NIV) *"Come now, let us settle the matter," says the Lord. "Though your sins are like scarlet, they shall be as white as snow; though they are red as crimson, they shall be like wool.*

My Mom, My Hero

A hero is someone who is ideal
Someone who is admired
Someone who still gives of themselves
Even when they are so tired.

I was thinking if there was anyone
Who I would want to be like
It would be my mom
My, hero, in this life.

I see the choices that she's made
I always felt so loved
She worked and never quit
She refused to give up.

She did what she had to do
Putting her family before herself.
I've always hoped I could do the same
If it were her cards I was dealt.

If you asked her
She would say,
"Oh, there are things that I would change."

But I guess if you asked any good mom
That's probably what she'd say.

Our mom worked to give us
The best life that she could
Putting her desires aside
So our lives could be good.

Our family's still in tact today
Because of the sacrifices that she made.

My mom dished out the "tough love"
She didn't take the easy way
She carried the heavy loads by herself
But she didn't run away!

One thing that is sure
She taught us what was right
And all three of us would say
For 'us' she'd be willing to fight!

We should give honor
Where honor is due
My Love, Admiration and Appreciation
Mom, all of these go to you.

Psalm 56:3 (KJV) What time I am afraid, I will trust in Thee.

No matter what you're going through …if you will speak God's word over your problem and take it to Him in prayer, He will turn it around for your good.

Romans 8:28 (KJV) All things work together for good to them that love God and are called according to His purpose.

We are all tempted to complain or talk about our problems, but what I have experienced is that it never really helps and usually makes you feel worse, because as we rehearse it and replay it, we're actually magnifying our problem. If we choose to rehearse God's word (His promises) over our problems, taking His advice, we are magnifying Him. That's what will change the problem.

Psalm 15:23 (KJV) A man has joy by the answer of his mouth.

There is nothing wrong with sharing with a friend or someone to get counsel, but it is very important that the counsel we are getting always lines up with God's word.

READ Psalm 34*

This Is What I'll Say

When I am afraid, this is what I'll say, "Lord, I trust in You to get me through whatever comes my way."

When I feel I'm all alone
And I don't know what to do
When I'm feeling overwhelmed
And really frazzled too.

I will simply stop and tell You
How I need Your help
If I put my problems in Your hands
I know all will be well.

You are the ONLY One
Who knows just what to do
You know what I need before I ask
But the problem must be brought to You.

Once it's in Your hands
You can begin to work
When we don't get God involved
Things just don't seem to work.

Listen very closely
He'll tell you what to do
The answer can come in many ways
Just trust Him, He'll lead you.

It could come as a thought
Or come from a book or a friend
You must do only what He tells you
So, this problem can come to an end.

Sometimes it may not be overnight
But the timing's not up to you
Just trust that He's God – He's all knowing
And He only wants the best for you.

What happens in the schools or the economy
In our Country or in our homes
When God is taken out - We're doomed!
You would think by now, we'd know!

It was trust in God from the very beginning
That birthed our nation and our faith.
Now it's built on lies and corruption
Instead of love - it's mostly hate.

We must get back to trusting Him
For things to turn out right
Whether it's our nation
Or in our personal lives.

There are many things in this life
That will make us feel afraid,
Do what you can, leave the rest up to God.
Then, "I trust You" that's what we should say.

Psalm 56:3-4 (NIV) When I am afraid, I put my trust in You.

Oh, September Morning

Oh, September morning
There's something in the air
I can't put my finger on it
But, I'm sure that it is there.

I feel as though there's something happening
Something I cannot see
I'm trusting that it will be good
That God's been preparing for me.

So, I'll just wait with expectancy
As the days play out ahead
Knowing that I'm in good hands with God
Lord, by Your Spirit – help me be led.

Visit them while they're well....

Send them flowers before they die.

(In the middle – before my miracle)
Just when I thought it couldn't get any worse!

On February 2017, I found out that we owed several thousands of dollars to the IRS. I was supposed to get back about $800. It never came. I called and that's when I found out we owed for years 2011, 2012, 2013, all of which I thought had been paid (another surprise). They put my income tax return toward those years. I really needed that money. I was working as much as I possibly could. I was working 40 hours a week, doing my brothers reports at night and cleaning a few houses on the side. (with the help of my mom and sister). Every dime of my paycheck went towards my house payment. I never called it "rent." In my heart it was still MY house. MY home. I did not have any extra money to pay the IRS, but if I did not pay, they would garnish my wages. I did not know what to do. I was at work when I got this call from the IRS. When I got off the phone I was just sitting there. I had no idea what I was going to do. I guess it was all over my face. My boss walked through and asked me if I was OK. I told her the situation, and she said, "Let's pray." She sat down beside me and took my hand and prayed with me about my situation. I am truly blessed to have a boss that is so good to me and that would pray for me! God was so sweet to have placed me here at this job during this very difficult time in my life. It is a safe place for me and I've been surrounded by so many wonderful people. A place of refuge while I healed. **I am so grateful.**

Over the next few months, the IRS granted me "innocent spouse relief," which lowered the taxes owed considerably. Then, someone that knew about my situation told me they wanted to take care of the rest of it.

On August 21, 2017, the remaining taxes were PAID IN FULL.

……but you say you love me.

We started our journey 24 years ago
And you promised me a ring.
It was only supposed to be two weeks
But this ring I've never seen.

Through the years I've spent
So much time alone.
At football games, family gatherings
Anniversaries….alone even at home.

……but you say you love me.

There have been times I was devastated
By unexpected news.
Like our property being up "for sale"
Or being humiliated at the bank drive thru.

There were certain things you were responsible for.
But you didn't follow through.
It cost us our credit and our security
You left me car-less for years too.

…..but you say you love me.

You've barely acknowledged me
The last several years.
No time for coffee, a movie or food.

Then it's time for you to leave for so long
But there are just harsh words between me and you.

.....but you say you love me.

While you're away, you forget to call back.
You said you were reading and time slipped away.

When it's been four days since we've talked
Your response, "I knew I'd talk to you on Monday."

When we had a chance to talk,
You said, "Let's talk later."

.....but you say you love me.

It seems as though there's nothing left
By the things you say and do.
The last was the most hurtful yet
There was only ONE ticket to Scotland, not TWO.

.....but you say you love me.

What kind of love is this?

~ ~ ~ ~ ~

Re: Oklahoma "Critical Care " Paramedic arrested.
On news 4-13-15

NEWS – THERE AND READY!

You were there and ready
To watch him fall!
You were there and ready
So we would see it all!

All on the 6 and 10 o'clock news
Humiliate others
So (who) could look good?

You were there and ready
To post the news
Of a good man while he's down
Shame on you!!!

Where was the news
When he went to school
To learn to save lives
So he could help all of you.

Where was the news
When he taught so many
To help others like he does
In the country – In the city.

He could have saved your mom, your cousin, your friend.
Or helped your uncle, your grandpa, your gran.

Where were you
When he saved that life?
You were probably sleeping
It was the middle of the night?

Nowhere to be found while he did something good.

BUT…

You were there on the spot
When the handcuffs went on.
You were there when they took him
And posted his "mug shot."

Does that make you great
For only posting BAD news
About a good man.
Have you walked in his shoes?

Have we become like animals
That we prey on the weak
Instead of helping the hurting
At least back to their knees.

Why don't we run to see why they are sad
And help them get up before it gets really bad.
But instead, we kick a good man
While he's down.
And spread his BAD news
All over town.

When's the last time
That you made a mistake?
Is the news how we'll know you?
How we'll recognize your face.

I know you have to report
What is going on.
But do we have to lose good values
In the middle of it all?

Look for the good – not just the bad.

Sometimes I find myself complaining, instead of being thankful. There is always something to be thankful for. Sometimes we have to look really hard. Sometimes we just need to be reminded…have a new perspective.

I am a person that would prefer to be up and moving and outside rather than sitting at a computer. I found myself complaining about what I had been asked to do. What was I thinking! A lot of the time what we are doing is a privilege. Having a job working for a great boss, being a mother, doing something that is in your heart.

Be thankful to God in whatever you're doing. Do everything as unto the Lord. Be willing to do what God is leading you to do today.

(NIV) Colossians 3:23 Whatever you do, work at it with all your heart, as working for the Lord….

My prayer…

Thank you, Lord, for using me…

It's an honor and a privilege
To write down what You say.
Forgive me for the complaining I've done
In the past – up to today.

For what you've given, should be respected
You give me such hope
When You speak – I'll say, "yes."
Instead of saying, "no."

The Value of a Snicker Bar

The value of the "little things" should
never be overlooked....

I was talking to my son's friend
Who is now in the Marines.
He still calls after all these years
He'll never know what it means.

Even though he is a friend
We consider him family.

He was telling me of a gift he received
Before Christmas – and what it means.
It was a Snicker bar
That was left anonymously.

I could tell it meant a lot to him
I saw the "tender" through the "tough."
It said to him, "he was appreciated"
And that he was simply "just thought of."

As we talked,
I compared things in my mind.
It's the little things that mean so much
That add a lot to someone's life.

I told him – his calls are like his Snicker bar
He chuckled – but understood.
We both knew the value of the "little things"
And that they should never be overlooked.

*If you have the thought to do something nice for someone
no matter how small or insignificant it may seem, do it.
You never know what it will mean to that person.*

The little things in life MEAN SO MUCH!

Darkest before the dawn....

The darkest moment
before the dawn……

My husband of 25 years left me two days after our 25th anniversary (June 9, 2017). I was devastated. All of our difficulties you have read about, he left me with and just walked away. I haven't heard from him since, no call, no text, no email…….*nothing.*

He left a note saying, "You wanted your freedom, you got it." To this day, I don't know what he meant by that. Leaving me in the condition that he left me in was not freedom. It was devastation. I didn't know if I could bear it.

BUT….

with God, being my strength, I was able to!

THE DARKEST MOMENT BEFORE THE DAWN

Just when I thought
It couldn't get any darker,
That day DID come.

It was definitely my darkest moment.
The darkest before the dawn.

....

I'm out working in the yard.
My husband's mother drives up with a note.
As I open it and read the first line,
A huge lump forms in my throat.

At that moment, my world came crashing in.
My husband was gone....
He said he'd never be back again.

The first line said,
"You always wanted to be free"
To this day....
I still don't know what he means.

We were married 25 years
And we've had our ups and downs.
But, I never saw this coming
My world came crashing down.

Not only did he leave,
Something I never thought he'd do.
He didn't even say, "Good-bye" or, "You did this" or
"I hate you."

He didn't give me a chance
To say what was on my heart.
In some ways, it's worse than death
The way he chose to part.

He said he always loved me
But he hurt me in so many ways.
If that is love, I'll do without
That kind of love – is pain.

Not only did he leave
But left me drowning as he left.
With $24 to my name
With unpaid bills and so much debt.

To me, the thing that hurts the most
Is that he would've let us starve.
If it weren't for our friends and family
Or that humiliating "food stamp" card.

There were times before he left
We didn't have much to eat.
Instead of working like he said,
I would see he and his mom go out to eat.

I don't know how he could do that
Knowing I was doing without.
Then it became obvious to me.
For a long time, he'd wanted out.

For years he would go places
While I just stayed at home,
But when it came time for me to go
There was no money, so I couldn't go.

As much as this has hurt
And so deep is the wound.
If he didn't love me anymore than this
Maybe this is for the good.

It's been four months since he up and left,
But God has been faithful through it all.
He's provided what we needed
He did not let us fall.

I'm so grateful for the help from
My friends and family
I pray God blesses them a "hundred fold"
For all they've done for me.

I may never know
The reason why he left,
But I know if I keep trusting God
My life, He'll always bless.

~~~
~~~

A Shattered Heart

When something happens
That you don't understand that shatters your heart
So severely it is sand.

~ There are no pieces left to put it together again. ~

Hope that was there
Now seems suddenly all gone.
It just slipped away
How do you hold on?

What you trusted so much
Just walked away.
How was it so easy?
Why didn't they stay?

~To be cast aside as though you were nothing.
Leaves a wound that's so painful, so deep, unrelenting.~

For someone to say
They love you and love God
Then lie, hurt and leave
That's nothing, but WRONG.

The only answer is that
They were deceived
It's in His word and it's clear to see.

You should love your wife
As Christ loved the church
And instead of your wants
Your family should come first.

Even if God asked you
To do something for Him
He wouldn't have you leave them
In a condition so "grim."

If we have to give an account
For every "idle word" we say
What else will we give an account for
On that "Judgement Day."

He said liars won't enter
The Kingdom of Heaven
...and not providing for your household,
"worse than an infidel" is mentioned.

The only way to victory
Is to stay on the path.
The path that God has chosen.
Not a path filled with wrath.

You can't make things happen
It's God's timing. You must wait!
IT'S HIS PLAN – NOT OURS
He's not too early or too late.

~~ ~~ ~~

Know that God is the only one
Who won't let you down
His blessings will be
Where obedience is found.

God is the only one
Who can piece back every part.

Of your brokenness,
Your hopelessness,
And your **Shattered Heart.**

FATHER, I WANT TO CHOOSE YOU

Father, I choose You
Over everything else
Over everything else
I choose You.

I choose You over being anxious
I choose you over being sad
I choose You over all temptation
I choose You over being mad.

I choose You over every thought
That exalts itself above You
I choose You to be my victory
I choose You to be my breakthrough.

I choose You to be my strength
My guide, when I don't know which way to go
I choose You to counsel me.
There's just so much that I don't know.

I choose You to comfort me.
When I am feeling low.
I choose you to lift me up
To lift my sad and weary soul.

There aren't many sure things in this life.
But one thing I know to be true.
There is only one who is trustworthy
And that's You, Father.
I choose You.

"PAIN"

What name does your pain have?
(All pain....different names)

What is the pain
That you're feeling right now?
Is it a lost love?
The loss of a spouse?

I sit here and think
Of each person I know
I see "pain's" left its mark
With its powerful blow.

I've seen depression in most
I've seen loneliness and shame.
All effects from this "pain"
Just disguised – different names.

I've seen anger, resentment
Unfaithfulness and, yes, hate.
The length "pain" goes to get to us...
But, now for some it's too late.

Some reach for something
To heal the wounds.
Some reach for drugs
Some reach for booze.

Some reach for the comfort of another
Instead of the ONE THING that can help you
recover.

Some think the answer
Is running away.
Getting a divorce
Even robbing a bank!

None of these things will heal your pain
They just make things worse
In so many ways!

Jesus said,
"I AM THE WAY, THE TRUTH
And the LIFE"
I can heal EVERY PAIN
That's why I died.

I saw your pain
While I hung on the cross.
Please, come to Me
Or you'll always be lost.

You've tried for so long
To live life without Me.
I soooooo love you.
Why can't you see!

This pain comes from someone
Who wants to destroy your soul.
He weakens you with "pain"
Then leads you down the wrong road.

I will heal your pain
I'll lift you up high.
I'll wrap you in love
And hug you real tight.

I'll walk with you
Hand in hand.
"Pain" will no longer control you
If, with Me, you will stand.

I'm not saying,
You'll never feel "pain"
But, you won't be its slave
Because "pain," I have slain.

I conquered sickness and sin
And pain on the cross.
Let Me be your Shepherd
Come to Me
Don't stay lost.

Shepherd – To watch over carefully, guide, lead and take care of.

John 10:11-18 (NIV) "I am the Good Shepherd. The good shepherd lays down his life for the sheep...

ONLY YOUR LOVE SOFTENS THE HEART

What has happened to me?
My heart is so hard.
Is it just selfishness?
Or life inflicted scars?

I don't want to be inconvenienced
By the needs of someone.
Someone who takes advantage
Who causes frustration and hurt.

Then I'm QUICKLY reminded
What's been done for me.
When Jesus was inconvenienced
And went to Calvary.

I clearly didn't get
what I deserved.
Instead, He forgave me
And gave me His love.

If I am to truly follow Him
I must love the way He loves.
Sometimes it is a fight within me
I don't think the way He does.

He says, "love your enemies."
"Do good to those who hate you."
"Bless those that curse you."
"Pray for those who mistreat you..."

Yes, it's true
We think so differently.
But, I choose to follow You
Instead of my selfish ways.

I do know, I'll need Your help with this.
Probably EVERDAY.
Let Your love soften my heart,
So I can love "like you do" today.

My heart breaks...at me.
Forgive me, Oh, Lord.

ONLY YOUR LOVE SOFTENS THE HEART

Luke 6:28, Matthew 16:24 (NIV)

The ones who are "there"
Are the ones who "care."

One of the things I've come to notice over the years is that the ones who "truly care," are the ones that are "there."

There are those that say, I'll always be there or I'll do anything I can to help, but when that time comes, they're nowhere to be found. I hate to admit it, but I have been guilty of this.

"Now, there are those situations that prevent us from being there. It just can't be helped.

~~ ~~ ~~

I'm sure you can recall hearing these words at some point in your life: "I was going to call, but..."
"I would have been there, but..."
I was going to do this, but..."

Don't give people your "buts," give them "you."

It does make me think of those people in my life who are "there"...and a lot of those times, I didn't even ask. (I want to be that kind of person.)

When you're happy and celebrating,,,,,,. . . who is "there"?
When you are sad and lonely, who is "there"?
When you just need to talk, who is "there"?
When you have a need, who is "there"?

THANK GOD EVERYDAY
FOR THOSE PEOPLE IN YOUR LIFE.

....the ones who are "there."

What if….

WE JUST FORGAVE

What if we forgave the one
That hurt us so many times.
Or the one that walked out on us
Just leaving us behind.

What if we forgave the one
That cheated – who was untrue.
Or the one that took advantage
And so easily lied to you.

What if we forgave
All the harsh words that were said.
The ones that were so painful
The ones we can't forget.

What if we forgave that one
Who has not been there for us.
The one who has lied to us
The one who lost our trust.

What if…

We stopped wallowing in self pity
And would be a blessing to someone.
What if we accepted God's forgiveness
For the "wrongs" that we have done.

What if we forgave ourselves
For what we've not become.
And started today to be "our best"
And chose to stay and not to run.

Get all things right before God.
Forgive them and He will forgive you
For all the wrong things you have done.

What if we forgave
How differently things would be.
Things would be better
For you and for me.

I wonder what our family would be like
How we would feel about each day
If we would simply forget the past
If we just loved – If we just forgave.

If we ask God to forgive us
That's simply what He does
Why is it so hard for us
So hard for us to love.

It's because we don't meet with Him
And let him fill us up
With His love, that is perfect
We come up empty, then just give up.

Unforgiveness holds us captive
By invisible chains
When we choose to forgive
Those chains begin to break.

We don't have to allow someone
To continue to hurt us.
But for us to be free
We must forgive them first.

I see it simply as a choice
That each of us can make
To be obedient to Him
We MUST forgive,
Because HE FORGAVE.

Matthew 6:15 (NIV)
But if you do not forgive others their sins, your
Father will not forgive your sins.

~ GOOD ENDING PENDING ~

To be continued in 3rd book....

Pain Is the Ink

Sometimes *Pain Is the Ink*
Used to write a song or a poem
Sometimes no other ink can be used
To turn another's pain into joy.

For it's the experience of one
That can show another
A different way to go.

How can we help someone
If we've never been there?
How else would we know?

This ink is an expensive ink
It comes at a very high price.
Usually there is great loss
Perhaps possessions or someone's life.

It is very painful to be the holder of this ink
You don't want it at the time.
But it might ease someone else's pain
Maybe change someone's life.

There comes a time
When the ink is all gone
There's no writing left to do.

If you can help others
With the words you write
Then the pain was worth going through.

Sometimes…

Pain Is the Ink

God proved to me that He is always trustworthy.

He did the impossible in my life.

He didn't walk away.

He didn't leave me.

I trusted Him.

He came through for me.

Even now, looking back over the past few years and seeing what he has done for me. Things that only He could do. It still amazes me.

Thank you, my sweet Heavenly Father.

Printed in the United States
By Bookmasters